South West Dreamers

Edited By Georgia Harris-Love

First published in Great Britain in 2017 by:

Young Writers
Remus House
Coltsfoot Drive
Peterborough
PE2 9BF
Telephone: 01733 890066
Website: www.youngwriters.co.uk

FOREWORD

Welcome to 'Once Upon A Dream – South West Dreamers'.

For our 'Once Upon A Dream' competition, we invited primary school pupils to delve within their deepest imaginations and create poetry inspired by dreams. They were not limited to the dreams they experience during their sleep, they were free to explore and describe their dreams and aspirations for the future, what could inspire a dream, and also the darker side of dreams... the nightmare!

The topic proved to be hugely popular, with children dreaming up the cleverest, craziest and, sometimes, creepiest of poems! The entries we received showcase the writing talent and inspired imaginations of today's budding young writers.

Congratulations to James Wood, who has been selected as the best poet in this anthology, hopefully this is a dream come true! Also a big well done to everyone whose work is included within these pages, I hope seeing it published help you continue living your writing dreams!

Georgia Harris-Love

CONTENTS

Malmesbury CE Primary School, Tetbury Hill

Pippa Hibbard (9)	46
Elise Davies (10)	48
Niamh Violet Jensen-McCarthy (9)	50
Millicent Constantina Bryar (9)	52
Nteasie Amankwa (10)	53
Isabelle Constable (10)	54
Chloe Hemmings (10)	55
Elliot Webb (10)	56
Annabelle Wreford-Bush (8)	57
Mia Doman (9)	58
Dan Eldridge-Lynch (9)	59
Ben Wilcox (10)	60
Clareece Loft (9)	61
Stephanie Jane Michelle Davidson (10)	62
Bobby Muttock (9)	63
Toby Poole (9)	64
Elsie Scanlon (11)	65
Jamie Ray Goldstone (10)	66
Amber Richards (10)	67
Tyler Matthew Moore (8)	68
Poppy Wadsworth (10)	69
Isabel Carrick (9)	70
Bailey Wicks (10)	71
Isabel Norman (9)	72
Henry Young (8)	73
Josh Slade (8)	74
Milo Chilman (9)	75
Declan Rice (9)	76
Matthew Norman (9)	77
Chloe Carol Kuchczynski (9)	78
Freya Willis (9)	79
Eloise Wilson (9)	80
Jodie Sarine Foster (9)	81
Joseph Sladden (8)	82
Ben Templer (10)	83
Laura Tate (9)	84
Harry Jacob White (8)	85
Rosie Katya Coode (10)	86
Joseph Kirkman (9)	87
Emily Holt (10)	88
James William Legg (9)	89
Charlie Hancock (9)	90
Macy May Ford (8)	91
Edward Lane (9)	92
Rosemary Joan Robins (9)	93
Lily Harris (9)	94
Fiona Hunt (9)	95
Samuel Davies (9)	96

Mitton Manor Primary School, Tewkesbury

Lauren Howe (10)	97
Amber Keightley (10)	98
Holly Greening (10)	100
Brooke Keay (10)	101
Jake Rowden (10)	102
Phoebe Kinsey (10)	103
Evie Marie Rowlands (10)	104
Robyn Smith (9)	105
Megan Rainbow (10)	106
Hannah Dyke (10)	107
Holly Stark (9)	108
Wil Redfern (10)	109
Amelia Hyldon (10)	110
Katie Wheeler (10)	111
Thomas Clements (9)	112
Evie Chambers (10)	113
Sophie Parker (10)	114
Evie Lawley (9)	115

Shrivenham CE Primary School, Shrivenham

Elsa Bearman (10)	116
Flora Waymouth (8)	118
Arun Dhoot (9)	119
Charlie Taylor (9)	120
Nyah Harmer (8)	121
Daniel Chaston (8)	122

Stonar School, Atworth

Bonnie Davies (9)	123
Laura Sparrow (9)	124
Isabella Beatrice Chadwick (9)	126
Poppy May Sumner (9)	128
Lilly Cherry (9)	130
Emma Louise Skinner (9)	131
Michael Ross Matthew MacLeod (9)	132
Eva Norman (9)	134
Phoebe Tombs (8)	135
Oliver Newman (8)	136
Oliver Deakin (9)	137

Stow On The Wold Primary School, Stow On The Wold

Lily Jennings (9)	138
Maggie Brain (8)	140
Oliver Hicks (8)	142
Madisen Keyte (9)	143
Luke Michael Smith (8)	144
Amelia Liljana Ruby Taylor (8)	145
Edward Nicholds-Brown (8)	146
Lexi Ellen Huckson (8)	147
Issy Bayliss (8)	148
Solly Bell (8)	149

Sturminster Marshall First School, Sturminster Marshall

Jacob Reed (8)	150
Constance Springett (8)	151
Hana Brittain (7)	152
James Mounty (8)	153
Edwyn White (8)	154
Freya Mabey (8)	155

Westrop Primary School, Highworth

Poppy Howarth-Barnes (11)	156
Chloe May Jones (11)	157
Jamal Alan Frost (11)	158

THE POEMS

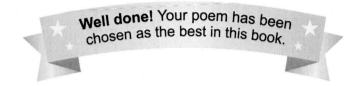

Well done! Your poem has been chosen as the best in this book.

Out Of The Darkness

Out of the darkness you will see,
a monster appeared to follow me,
it followed me as I walked my dog,
it followed me through the rain and fog,
it followed me home and up to my room,
it cast a grey shadow as big as the moon,
I tried to reach out and touch it with my hand,
but before I could it turned to sand,
I looked down at the floor and all I could see,
was a pile of red raging eyeballs staring at me.
I could not believe what was happening right then,
I glanced up at the clock and it said half-past ten,
I felt a warm hand stroke across my forehead,
It was my mum, I was actually safe in my bed!

James Wood (9)
Malmesbury CE Primary School, Tetbury Hill

The Mystic Underworld

I dreamt in bed about an underworld
Where Ted, Finlay and I were spawned
In the mystic underworld, there were weird creatures,
That were natural, evil but friendly.
The year was 5017, it was the future,
Dragons with three heads (Hydra)
Until a monster called Chagarath came, he could talk
He was red, furious, he'd always been mad
We all tried defeating him.
We had defeated him...

Kenzi Eligh Slade (9)

Sweet Nightmare

My sweet dreams drift away,
A draught around my feet,
The darkness fills my head,
But still I am asleep,
Rushing round and round,
Devil playing chase
Memories flooding back,
But still I do not wake
The wind is blowing hard,
Spinning in my head,
Trees are upside down
But there I lay in bed.
My feet don't touch the ground
I'm falling through the air,
Looking all around,
But something makes me stare,
A bed appears from nowhere,
Could it really be?
Suddenly I get there,
The covers of safety,
Deep in the distance,
There's a calling from afar,
It's a warm sweet voice that calls me,
'School time Natasha!'

Natasha Webb (10)
Charter Primary School, Chippenham

Safe With My Mum

I had a nightmare last night,
It was so scary,
I'm going to puke, well I might,
I hope I never have a dream so scary.

I had a nightmare last night,
My brilliant brother was with me,
He was terrified that scary night,
He's never been so scared with me.

I had a nightmare last night,
My best friend was with me,
She was terrified that scary night,
She's always been scared with me.

I had a nightmare last night,
My mum was with me,
She was terrified that scary night,
But I felt safe when she was with me.

Ayla Hosking (10)
Charter Primary School, Chippenham

The Land I Call My Own

The land I call my own
I entered it, well at least I didn't moan
At first I thought I'd break a bone,
Then I figured how birds roam.
As I walked down the path,
I thought I might take a bath,
I looked up to the sky,
And there I was flying high,
As I looked down below was a king in a castle
I thought I'd give him hassle,
A clown ran down to me with an evil grin across
his face
Running like Usain Bolt it started to give chase,
As I fell to the ground, I found myself safe in bed,
And realised it was all in my head.

Lara King (10)
Charter Primary School, Chippenham

The Mystical Portal

Lost in an extinct kingdom
My best friends stand by my side.
I feel scared.
But together we are brave.
Searching for a portal that will get us out.
Until a magical mist appears as a beacon of hope.
The mist scatters in the air.
A shadow appears that looks like a pointy hat and
long robe.
A kind wizard offers to help us.
With his shaft he draws a portal that we need to find.
There are two islands that need to be saved
On one island there is a spider down in a cave.
On another island there is a dragon, dinosaur
and monster.

Ryan David Sanders (10)
Charter Primary School, Chippenham

Hungry For A Football

Looking at this strange blue ground,
I have been wondering what on earth I've found,
There, right at my feet
Is a ball made of meat!
I kick it high, then I kick it low,
I don't know where this will go,
In the goal I see a river,
Suddenly I start to shiver,
I shoot as fast as a racing wagon,
Then out the river pops a dragon!
He uses his fire to cook the meat,
Then it's all ready for him to eat,
I think this is so funny,
I suddenly wake up to see my mummy!

Freddie Wyn Riley (10)
Charter Primary School, Chippenham

Dreams, Oh Dreams

Dreams, oh dreams, I love to dream
I dream of gardens and flowers that beam.
Dreams, oh dreams, some are scary
like a big, fat monster that looks really hairy
Dreams, oh dreams, I dream of big stars
Like Whitney Houston who drove posh cars
Dreams, oh dreams, they don't waste your time
especially the dreams that involve crime!
Dreams, oh dreams, they're sometimes plain
like when you dream of a football match, now that's
pretty lame!

Abigail McDonald (10)
Charter Primary School, Chippenham

Nightmare

Nightmares, nightmares in my head
It feels like ghosts are in my bed
The room is dark and cold,
The walls look like they're going to fold,
I clutch my blanket and hold it tight,
Because I know I'm in for a frightful night
I go to sleep and close my eyes,
And now dream of butterflies,
I wake up in the morning to bright sunshine,
I now know that everything will be fine.

Jack James Burchell (10)
Charter Primary School, Chippenham

FA Cup Final

One night I had a dream,
To play for my favourite team,
Arsenal is the team for me,
Because they always finish in the top three.
I dreamt I played in the FA Cup,
I scored a goal, I was well made up,
I put it to the goalie's right,
He dived but I was well out of sight.
Celebrating the goal I scored that night.

Lewis Paul Young (9)
Charter Primary School, Chippenham

My Unicorn

My unicorn whose hair is pink.
She poos candy and it doesn't stink.
She likes to fly up in the cloud,
This makes me really proud.

The candy she poos is very sweet,
It's what my friends and I love to eat!
My unicorn loves rainbow-coloured butterflies,
She likes to sing them a lullaby.

Alisha Birkett (10)
Charter Primary School, Chippenham

My Football Life

Football is about having fun
Being part of a team
Scoring, tackling, kicking the ball
I see the football flying through the air,
straight into the goal
Mum and Dad cheering and shouting like mad.
Football can be rough but not all the time,
It's all about taking part and having fun.

Keatton Nicholas Cole (10)
Charter Primary School, Chippenham

Clowns

C razy and mischievous

L oud and happy

O ver exaggerated

W eird and wonderful

N aughty and extreme.

Riley Dean Fisher (10)

Charter Primary School, Chippenham

Once Upon A Dream...

Once upon a dream,
I open my eyes and behold,
A fantasy land,
A mystical world,
Like I'm in Heaven, just not dead.

Once upon a dream,
I cast my eye on a glittering scene
A gleaming sky,
A beaming sun,
I feel lost, alone but strangely delighted.

Once upon a dream,
I hear a flutter of wings,
I see a flash of sparkling silver,
An angel maybe,
Or something else.

Once upon a dream,
A gleaming figure stands before me
Its beauty takes over me,
I hear its soft voice,
I feel its warm hand on my skin,
But I'm drifting away into a deep, endless sleep.

Maisie Shepherd (11)
Crudwell CE Primary School, Malmesbury

The Darkness

A dream that is light and sunny;
Beautiful, crisp, clear water.
A boat,
The bow ploughs through the vast blue oceans.

Then suddenly, yet almost slowly,
The boat plunges into an inky darkness.
Then blackness,
Stretching as far as the eye can see.

Heavy is the blackness,
So heavy I can almost feel it,
Pressing down on my shoulders.

Then an island in the distance small at first,
But bigger, closer, blacker.
Within seconds, a black towering fortress:
The boat won't stop.
On and on it goes,
Until suddenly, it hits!

Ellie Barlow (11)
Crudwell CE Primary School, Malmesbury

The Unknown!

Once upon a dream,
I was falling, falling, falling,
Once upon a dream
It seemed so long ago.

Collapsing, plummeting, down I go,
On and on, more and more - oh no!
All around me - darkness and despair,
Eerie smoke, a flash of light, a sudden flare
Followed by a creature - an unknown,
I realise I am not alone.

A cold, icy, mythless laugh,
It came, it came from afar,
A glint of red, crimson red light,
Sinister and evil but bright,
Was it human or was it not?
I had not a clue, not a jot!

Freddie Williamson (11)
Crudwell CE Primary School, Malmesbury

Nightmare

My dreams are always bad,
I have never had a good one,
I dread going to bed,
Because inside my head,
There's a different land of darkness.

Sometimes it would be monsters,
The next it would be clowns,
But they're not that bad,
Compared to the ones I have.

On the worst of nights it would be,
The same dream over again,
It all starts off fine,
Walking along the river it's beautiful
Then I fall in,
I start to fall down,
Further than I ever fell before.

Imogen Baker (11)
Crudwell CE Primary School, Malmesbury

The Future (I Hope!)

Looking up at silver towers, looming overhead
Glistening in the moonlight, beacons shining red.
Flying cars take to the sky,
Ninety miles per hour,
Breaking limits as they fly,
Throttle on full power.
Whilst down below, inside a house,
A robot paints the door,
Then comes inside to feed the mouse,
And goes and mops the floor.

This future place, this world of ease,
It really is quite cool,
But now it's time for me to wake,
And head off to my school...

George Whelan (10)
Crudwell CE Primary School, Malmesbury

My Football Dream

As the scouts watch
I play football
My dream of my career to sign for FGR
I play striker and I come on, we have a corner,
The ball is delivered into me, I think to myself
One ball, one jump, one goal
And I celebrate in happiness as I score
The final whistle blows and we win 1-0
The scout comes over
He gives me offers and the last offer on the page
is FGR.
My heart stops for a minute
And I sign for my dream club
But what's next for me?

Blyth Stewart (10)
Crudwell CE Primary School, Malmesbury

The Whales

Once upon a dream,
I was on the Lone Island,
No one's been before,
No one else was there either.

Or so I thought,
I took a stroll down to the water,
As clear as a million crystals,
I looked at the horizon and what did I see?

I saw a pod of whales,
Great beauties they were,
As they came closer, all I could do,
Was gaze at them like an eagle eyeing its prey
Before they turned and disappeared
I was never to see them again...

Avie David (10)
Crudwell CE Primary School, Malmesbury

The Maze

As I walked through the overgrown bushes of
the maze,
I heard something that made me shudder,
I heard a loud, high-pitched hiss that belonged to
a spider,
I chose to ignore this abnormal happening
And I carried on in hope of finding a way out,
A low groan suddenly filled the air
And sent an electric shock down my spine.
I heard a skitter scatter arriving behind me,
I started to run,
I fell,
I was awake and safe on my bedroom floor.

Daniel Gilbert (11)
Crudwell CE Primary School, Malmesbury

The Monsters

Every night when I go to bed I check for monsters,
the ones I dread.
Most of them have big sharp teeth,
that could eat you in one heartbeat.
They are always watching you,
even when you are on the loo.
When the devil lights are out,
they'll be there without a doubt,
watching you throughout the night.
Then I realise I was in my bed,
but now knowing the one thing I dread...

Zachary Hamilton (11)
Crudwell CE Primary School, Malmesbury

Monster

M y heart was racing, racing, racing, racing
O pposite me was a scary, scary monster
N othing could have prepared me for this
S cared, I took a small, small step back
T he monster showed his razor-sharp teeth
E ntering this dream was a bad, bad idea
R unning far, far away was not an option
S uddenly, I woke up in my cosy, cosy bed.

Sophie Bullock (11)
Crudwell CE Primary School, Malmesbury

Where Am I?

I've landed in this strange, strange land,
I don't know where I am,
There are purple trees, blue grass
And bunnies hopping backwards
I cannot see my feet,
There's mist all over the ground.
I take one step forwards,
Right onto a waiting cloud.
It takes me up, up, up,
Into the starry night sky
I get to my stop and off I hop,
Right into my waiting bed.

Elsa Nash (10)
Crudwell CE Primary School, Malmesbury

A Whole New World

I open my eyes,
To a whole new world,
A brand new life has been unfurled,
All around amazing smells,
Like the delicate scent of bluebells,
I look up and see,
Beautiful butterflies smiling at me,
Candyfloss clouds float by
As I raise my head up high,
What an incredible world I have entered in.

Sophia Tjolle (11)
Crudwell CE Primary School, Malmesbury

Lost With Unicorns

L ive in magnificent woods that would transform into animals

O ver the hills where grass could make your dreams come true

S uper sparkling horns lighting the blue sky

T ears coming as a waterfall from the sky, full with clouds.

W ater would help you find an unusual place if you were lost

I n the shining lake, fishes would dance to the wind's rhymes

T errific trees blowing in the powerful wind

H ouses would look at the trees strangely

U nique unicorns would fly up the sky gracefully

N ature could blend in with wildlife animals

I magination is the way you'll find the fountain of magic

C ars freaking out when seeing a splendid place

O bserving slowly you'll see people trying to find this creature

R acing as fast as dragons, they pulled their wings out in the gazing sun

N ight would fall down and the golden sun would go
to sleep

S himmering stars would glow in the pitch-black night
sky!

Miriam Diakite (9)
Even Swindon Primary School, Raybrook Park

Dream Of The Jungle

Dream of the jungle
What colours can you see?
Green, yellow, blue, brown,
Roar! like a lion,
Snap! like a crocodile,
Tweet! like a bird,
No need to be crazy,
Did you know monkeys are actually lazy.
Dream of the trees they are actually quite cool.
The leaves are as silky as sunshine
The palm tree is as shimmery as shine
The tropical talking toucan is as soft as silk...
But wait a minute my mind is taking me somewhere,
It is taking me to my bed where I keep all my
hidden dreams.

Nazeefa Ferdoush Taluckder (8)
Even Swindon Primary School, Raybrook Park

My Hopeful Dream

My dream,
To no longer see a bomb fall from a jet stream.
For no more viruses to take a life,
To come home to a loving wife.
For no more quakes caused by Earth's anger,
To no longer feel the need to use a dagger.
For equality worldwide,
To not become mortified,
By the starvation crisis,
And hope not to see anyone lifeless
To put a stop to pollution,
To find a solution
My dream
A possible one.

Matilde Ferreira (11)
Even Swindon Primary School, Raybrook Park

I Saw A Unicorn

Hello Unicorn!
What do you want to eat?
Do you wish for any corn or cereals?
I am in the forest.
Happy because I see a unicorn,
Happy to gather the beautiful flowers.
Suddenly I feel something,
An apple falls into my head,
Then I wake up and I am happy,
Because I felt and saw a fluffy unicorn,
Right in my arms.
I had held it in my arms very tightly,
I was happy to see a unicorn.

Ioana Bucuresteanu (8)
Even Swindon Primary School, Raybrook Park

I Dream Hard

I dream to dance.
I dream to sing.
I dream all the time
Because I dream
All my life.

When you dream you think of things
That makes you happy
Some make you sad
But when you try you will do it
No matter what.

I dream to sing
I dream to dance
I will never give up
No matter what!

Jasmine Sexbery (9)
Even Swindon Primary School, Raybrook Park

Babies, Friends, Love

B eautiful little babies lost in a small shop
A mazing little things, I saw one try to hop
B abies in a small shop, someone needs to buy them
I zzy the cross baby started to cry
E llie the angry baby started to scream
S ophie the massive baby wanted a drink.

F red the hungry baby screamed for a snack
R inga the good baby was quiet and still
I sabella the naughty baby took some snacks
E mily the little baby played with a small book
N atalie the funny baby just had a sneaky look
D an the crazy baby pretended to cook
S am the sleepy baby looked inside a small book.

L ily the strong baby saw a little snail
O lly the quiet baby saw a bluebird's tail
V icki the cute baby jumped inside the carriage
E llie the baby ate a small green cabbage.

Georgina Serjeant (7)
Greatfield Park Primary School, Up Hatherley

A Midsummer's Dream

In the enchanted forest I walked quietly and carefully.
I heard wolves howl and birds tweet.
Suddenly I saw purple and pink sparkles above
the treetops.
I followed the bright, beautiful light.
It led me to a lovely fairy with golden wings
called Shimmer.
Also a unicorn with a golden mane and tail.
She was called Mossy.
We walked together and found a letter
'Follow the map at the back to find me'
So we followed the map and found a beautiful palace.
A dog wearing a crown and her name was
Queen Titiana.
We gave her some new diamond wings
She tried to fly but... failed!

Izzobel Newman (8)
Greatfield Park Primary School, Up Hatherley

The Middle Of An Enchanted Forest

In the middle of my enchanted sleep, I have a
funny dream
It has a lot of colourful flowers.
Fairy dust with fairies whizzing by.
I am with Ronaldo, a famous football player,
A black pug with an elf costume on
And my best friend Isabelle.
We are in an enchanted forest.
Lots of fairy dust and flowers.
I feel excited and a bit nervous at the same time.
We find an ugly goblin.
I fall into a swamp.
We are up in a fairy kingdom with a fairy queen
I make friends with the fairy queen.
We get tossed in a world of dust
I end up locked up in a tower with my friends.

Libby Pitman (8)
Greatfield Park Primary School, Up Hatherley

Monster Flying By

M onsters, creepy things were everywhere
O n the pretty bed on the colourful table
N othing to grab them
S uddenly the window opened, I felt scared
T he scary things went out...
E legantly
R ushing out, I followed them.

F inally they stopped
L ying on a bench
Y ummy cakes walked by
I was so surprised
N ight-time came, I saw the monsters!
G ross! One was in the bin!

B in laughed all night
Y ummy cake flew by!

Izzy Cook (7)
Greatfield Park Primary School, Up Hatherley

The Race

I was riding a motorbike, friends quickly popped out.
We had a race.
Around the humongous hills
Through the forest
Back to the beach.
The race began at twelve o'clock
To the volcano
Suddenly boulders started to fall.
But we dodged them happily.
We carried on through the forest.
Didn't take long because it was a small forest and to the beach
Was not easy because people were in the way
Only one metre!
And they all tried and celebrated with cake.

James Abernethy (8)
Greatfield Park Primary School, Up Hatherley

Herobrine

I could only see palm trees
Noch, a green greedy goblin and Herobrine?
Me and my friends Cool Noah and Epic Theo
All stood in a line
We could only see green and small white dots like
Herobrine eyes.
We all shouted, 'Who's there?' and we heard a lie.
So we ran away in fright
But he was fighting after us shouting
Just as that happened
Noch the creator of Minecraft forests jumped out of a
tree and landed on Herobrine.

Max Clapham (8)
Greatfield Park Primary School, Up Hatherley

Magical Fairy

My imaginary fairy came to life
She broke her arm and gave me a fright
Where did she go?
Did she land in my old coat or in my bottle of Coke
Oh, there she is! I need to know what her name is?
Is she silky? Is she a ball?
No, no, no she is too cool
I wonder if she's a tooth fairy
I wonder if she's a knight
What a night I have had
'Sweet dreams,' she said to me.

Emily Faith Carroll (8)
Greatfield Park Primary School, Up Hatherley

Baby Land

B aby Land, there was a fluffy baby unicorn
A glistening, colourful forest
B aby Land was in the middle of the scary place
Y ou're on the moon, going to slip.

L ittle baby lost
A little magic dust was in the sky
N ow we're home at 57AD
D iapers to be washed in the washing machine.

Indie Bea Birt (7)
Greatfield Park Primary School, Up Hatherley

Unicorns

U nicorns high, unicorns low
N o one knew they were in my amazing room
I n every part they surrounded me
C louds creeping up on me
O ther people have got different unicorns too
R unning backwards with the unicorns
N o, this is very, very funny
'S oup!' said my mum, ready for an amazing lunch.

Chloe Speller (7)
Greatfield Park Primary School, Up Hatherley

Clowns

C lowns hunting on a starry night

L ost people walk when it is really bright.

O ats for sick, homeless people

W here are my spooky dino teammates?

N obody likes scary clowns, spooky dinos or fire
dragons that are evil

'S upper!' said my strong dad. 'Are you awake?'

Deedee Rose Ryerson (8)

Greatfield Park Primary School, Up Hatherley

Fairies, Fairies, Fairies

Fairies in my mind
I wake up sleepily
I see them alive
Look up to the sky at night
I'm not in my room anymore
I'm in an enchanted forest with my family of four
I meet the special fairies
They welcome me into their home
but I have to leave,
to the land of my life.

Niamh Pickersgill (7)
Greatfield Park Primary School, Up Hatherley

The Enchanted Forest

I was with Zoella and Isabelle
We were in the middle of the enchanted forest
We saw a rainbow unicorn being chased by a human
I could hear monkeys eating bananas
Something tapped me.
It was a beautiful golden fairy.
But then I woke up and it was my mum
Waking me up for school.

Chloe Charlotte Eva Maynard-Ramsay (8)
Greatfield Park Primary School, Up Hatherley

The Mysterious Island

Unicorn fly me to Maya the monkey
Oh no, the goblins took her
Fly high in the sky and we shall find the
missing monkey
We shall fly down like an eagle, got her!
Oh no, five minutes to dinner
We have to go through Candy Land
We made it, yum-yum!

Sofia Devereux-Renny (8)
Greatfield Park Primary School, Up Hatherley

My Family Dream

All of my family has a superpower,
My power is lightning
My mum has fire
My dad's power is super strength
My brother's power is to shrink and grow.
That was my dream.

Maximillian Joseph Lewinski (8)
Greatfield Park Primary School, Up Hatherley

Whizz, Pop, Bang!

Once upon a dream
I was with this girl called Latt,
Who saw a big black cat,
It walked from left to right,
'Is that Lucky?' Latt said
'No it is unlucky and don't start a fight!'

Whizz, pop, bang!
The teleportal rang,
And it sucked us right in

One look, there was a dino,
This was worse than seeing a rhino!
Suddenly a T-rex came up to us,
I looked at it, saw some pus,
Roar! it bellowed,
It was going to take a strike when,

Whizz, pop, bang!
The teleportal rang
And it sucked us in

'Where are we?'
'Can't you see?'
'We're in the future!'
'Oh, so we can make up words like Looture?'

'No!'
'At this moment you are turning into my foe.'
'Now that's not very nice.'

Whizz, pop, bang!
The teleportal rang
And it sucked us in.

'What are we wearing?'
'Now this is scaring...'
'Shush.'
Boom, boom, boom.
World War Two!
'What are you two doing here? You will be leaving soon!'
'No,' we replied
'You better start making boots or I will shoot!'

Whizz, pop, bang!
The teleportal rang
And it sucked us in

Where will it take you?

Pippa Hibbard (9)
Malmesbury CE Primary School, Tetbury Hill

Fear

Time to go to sleep, it was nine o'clock
It was getting late (*tick-tock, tick-tock*)
Leaping into the warmth of my safe, cosy bed
I rested my eyes and my poor weary head.

Flash!

I was in a street that was happy and bright.
The cobbled road shone, even at night,
A panther, dark as coal, rested a paw on my knee.
Still he wasn't dangerous, in fact as friendly as
could be.

Suddenly, the mood shifted
A dark feeling of evil lifted
Lightning flashed and thunder roared,
Round a corner there charged a horde.

Of townsfolk, their bodies glowing red,
With eyes that seemed to bore a hole through
my head,
They grabbed me and my panther friend,
And pushed us, forced us round the bend.

They led us around trees that seemed to mutter,
The trees hurled insults and my legs turned to butter,

Finally we arrived in a small clearing,
With a huge bonfire, and lots of people cheering.

Suddenly, they shoved us into the flames,
I closed my eyes, waiting for the pain
I opened them again and found I was in bed,
With my panther (actually a kitten) curled up by
my head.

Elise Davies (10)
Malmesbury CE Primary School, Tetbury Hill

Dinosaur

I've had a dream, I've had it before,
I was being chased by a dinosaur.

I wasn't alone, I was with my mates,
We were all wearing roller skates,
Being chased by a dinosaur.

We rolled far and wide,
Trying to find a place to hide,
Being chased by a dinosaur.

We came across a cave,
Which said: 'Property of Dave', whilst,
Being chased by a dinosaur.

Dave was the dinosaur,
I'm alone - It's now one not four,
Why am I being chased by a dinosaur?

And now it's just me,
Dave invited me in for tea.
Suddenly woke! My belly was rumbling and sore,
I'm no longer being chased by a dinosaur.

Turns out I was just hungry!
Time for toast and tea.

That's why I was being chased by a dinosaur!

Niamh Violet Jensen-McCarthy (9)
Malmesbury CE Primary School, Tetbury Hill

My Row With The Sea

Once upon a midnight's dream,
I was at sea, it was supreme!
On I rowed my little birch boat.
The sound of waves made a beautiful note.
Then, I felt a gentle breeze,
So I put up my sail to move with ease.

However, a tragedy ruined my plans,
When the sky turned grey, sweat ran from my hands!
I had never been alone in a storm before!
Vast waves flooded my boat, more and more.
A large wave approached - 'This is it,' I muttered.
It ran through my nose, I coughed and I spluttered...

Black. Silence. I am dead, but I'm not! I was thinking.
I thought I drowned, I was helplessly sinking!
I tossed and I turned at this mysterious thought.
If my name wasn't Millicent, I wouldn't have fought.

Millicent Constantina Bryar (9)
Malmesbury CE Primary School, Tetbury Hill

Imagine The Sweet Treats

See chocolate fountains and fall, rivers and ponds
A world of sweets and pleasant treats.
Dream-a-licious is the name
As it's written above me on a sugar cane.

I get shown around the place by my new best friend,
Their gleaming smile will never end.

My five best friends are there, by my side,
While my little pony trots around at night.

As I woke from my cotton candy bed,
Surprise I was to be in this land,
But amazing it is to enjoy every bit I had.

When I woke from my dream
I was keen to show kindness to the friends I knew,
And me, great powers of friendship I had inside,
But when I got out of bed, what did I see...?
A toffee on the floor in front of me.

Nteasie Amankwa (10)
Malmesbury CE Primary School, Tetbury Hill

The Clown

And now it's time, the curtains are shut,
Now my eyes have sealed like a cut.
It now is time to begin our dream,
From deep blue seas to a sunbeam.

And in a split second, we are at the fair,
Look, there's a tiger, and a grizzly bear,
But oh no sat in the corner,
Is a clown with a worm as a finger.

Now it's a nightmare, terror has struck
The clown is hiding at the hook-a-duck,
And now the bear has gone loose
The tiger is chewing on a goose.

I hope the ringmaster doesn't get me with glue
But now the curtains are open, phew,
It is now time to go to school
It will all be fine until bed starts to call.

Isabelle Constable (10)
Malmesbury CE Primary School, Tetbury Hill

Evil Unicorn

As light as a feather, I floated into the cloudy sky,
As I flew high I looked at my tiny house I
said, 'Goodbye,'
As I was surrounded by cloud, I wanted to start crying.
As soon as I stopped flying, I felt someone was spying.

I saw a horn and two deadly red eyes,
It was an evil unicorn I wanted to go home I was
so unwise.
The evil unicorn pounced, I ran, I screamed, I...
I woke up and I am in bed and I sigh.

But oh no I overslept,
It's ten o'clock, I'll get detention I expect.
I got in and my teacher was cross, she said I had
no respect.
So now I'm grounded, I told you, I was correct.

Chloe Hemmings (10)
Malmesbury CE Primary School, Tetbury Hill

Late For School

I'm running down the street because I'm late
for school,
Then suddenly my feet come off the ground.
I'm flying! I'm flying!
It's amazing, the cars are getting smaller
underneath me
The air is rushing through my hair,
People stop, look up and stare
Up ahead I see the school
I've just flown past the swimming pool!
Up and down like a roller coaster,
I fly to the school, it's getting closer
Just when I'm about to stop
My body falls and starts to drop!
I'm metres, inches from the ground,
My body spinning around and around
Then I wake up in my bed,
My body is safe and I'm not dead!

Elliot Webb (10)
Malmesbury CE Primary School, Tetbury Hill

Gymnastics Dream

G oing on I feel nervous

Y et I feel so nervous, my rival goes on

M eeting other gymnasts is so nerve-racking

N earer and nearer, soon it's my turn

A s my rival finishes I know it is my chance

S tepping out my nerves go away

T umbling across the mat doing my best skills

I know I am going to beat her

C lapping mad but I fall.

D own and down I go, feeling so sad

R ecovering well I spring back up

E nding my routine I feel okay

A pplause from the audience I feel surprised

M y gymnastics dream came true, I got gold!

Annabelle Wreford-Bush (8)
Malmesbury CE Primary School, Tetbury Hill

Magical Wood

I saw a fairy in the magical wood
Some people don't like them, but I think they are good.
I looked at her and she looked at me,
She was peeping down from the top of a very tall tree.
Her tights were dark green and her hair was
bright pink.
She smiled as she looked and gave me a wink!
My sister couldn't see her, nor could my dad.
They said I couldn't see her, but really I had.
I came back to the tree the very next day to find
her again.
And I would ask her to play but, she wasn't there
And all I could see was a sparkle of glitter up high in
the tree.

Mia Doman (9)
Malmesbury CE Primary School, Tetbury Hill

Sweet Dreams

S uddenly my eyelids drop, let the sweet dreams
begin.

W here am I?

E nchanted forest full of wonderful creatures

E xcited by all the smells and colours of the forest

T rees are talking to me, surely not!

D elightful bluebells ringing the bells on the forest
floor

R ivers are full of chocolate instead of water.

E xtremely tempted to go in the chocolate rivers

A nimals dancing to the tune of the bluebells

M aybe I will join in the dancing

S uch a sweet dream, I never want it to end.

Dan Eldridge-Lynch (9)

Malmesbury CE Primary School, Tetbury Hill

Footballer

F ans all around the stadium cheer
O pportunity of a lifetime here
O ffensive player meanly tackles a player
T he ref shouts, 'Off!' and a penalty is given
B all in hand 88th minute I step up to the spot
A ll around the stadium falls silent as I take my shot
L eft-footed, I boot the ball back of the net, the crowd all roars
L iverpool legend I will be as my goal means we lead the score
E nd of the game, the Champions League winners
R udely I'm woken up as my mum shouts, 'Dinner!'

Ben Wilcox (10)
Malmesbury CE Primary School, Tetbury Hill

Dragon Run

A flaming light,
A flashing blur,
Amazing sight,
A grumble stir,

And where am I? I wonder
Is this true and is it real?
I see a flash of thunder,
There's something that I feel,

Boom! Bash! A weird wild clash,
Is that a dragon I see?
Boom! Bash! I hear a smash!
It is a dragon I flee,

Are those spiders I see? Am I trapped?
Where should I run? Where should I go?
Then there is something that flapped,
Then I sat straight in my bed.
Oh? That was a dream though.

Clareece Loft (9)
Malmesbury CE Primary School, Tetbury Hill

The Utterly Ugly Unicorn

Once upon a time far, far away
Where a unicorn who liked to neigh
The place was very grey
But the moonlight shone
The pretty moonlight shone
But the other unicorns went a different way.

The unicorn was brown
And acted like a clown
But when you got to know him, he was very kind
Ugly but kind
Ugly but sweet
And he was pretty blind.

But then one amazing day
The unicorn ate some hay
All of a sudden he started to fly
He grew a beautiful mane
A colourful mane.
Then he turned into a real guy.

Stephanie Jane Michelle Davidson (10)
Malmesbury CE Primary School, Tetbury Hill

Murmurs

It starts with a flash,
and then he speaks to me.
I really do think, *just leave me be!*

You see where I'm going,
This is a bad dream.
At the start of it, there is a humongous beam.

When I was little,
It gave me a fright.
But as I got older, it gives me a bite.

The dream is called Murmurs,
because it does so.
I suppose he's a bit like a clown because of his big bow.
At the end of the dream,
He gives me a clover.
I wake up and say... 'I've had murmurs all over.'

Bobby Muttock (9)
Malmesbury CE Primary School, Tetbury Hill

The High Bounce

I climbed aboard my trampoline
and with a bend of my knees and a jump with my legs,
I rise up high above the treetops.

I keep bouncing high until I can fly with the birds
and bees.
I travel so high,
I keep going on and on and on, passing through the
blue sky,
and passing the plane, heading for the stars.
I see I'm going...

Suddenly I slow my brakes on fast.
I'm no longer on Earth, I've hit space.
I don't know when my adventure will end.
I just hope I'm back in time for bed.

Toby Poole (9)
Malmesbury CE Primary School, Tetbury Hill

The Staircase

In a dream anything could happen,
In a dream you could fly,
In a dream you could die,
But really in a dream anything could happen,
So in my dream it wasn't like a theme.
It's when you fly,
When you fly,
I flew down the staircase,
Not tripping on my shoe lace
Flying is great,
It's not something you can hate,
The best part was when I flew to the coast,
I liked that part the most,
Then I awoke,
With a bit of a choke,
Then I realised I could fly,
So I hoped I would not fall and die.

Elsie Scanlon (11)
Malmesbury CE Primary School, Tetbury Hill

Lost

T he trees rustle over my head
H orrifying sight in every direction
E ndless ways to turn, I'm praying they won't find me dead.

J ust then it starts, adrenaline kicks into action
U nannounced elephants charge through the mist
N ear death, heart pounding, I run for my life
G athering speed, my tired legs start to resist
L ooking for a place to hide, branches cut like a knife
E dging towards a cave, I crawl to the end and take my last breath.

Jamie Ray Goldstone (10)
Malmesbury CE Primary School, Tetbury Hill

I Don't Dream

I don't dream but I wait for the dreams that
never come.
As I lie in my bed I look at the alarm clock
Which is glowing in the dark room.
The pain spreads through me as I realise
There are hours and hours of dreamless sleep yet
to come.
The muffled sound of the television downstairs
Disturbs the thought of dreaming.
I close my eyes and there is nothing but darkness.
The next minute I open my eyes to find the
morning light
And a distant voice saying, 'Wake up, time for school!'

Amber Richards (10)
Malmesbury CE Primary School, Tetbury Hill

Monstrous Beast

S urfing in the glistening deep blue sea
H iding from the monstrous beast.
A great white shark thundered up to me
R azor-sharp teeth trying to snap me
K eeps on looking as if I'm his big tasty meal.

D iscovering my worst fear is here
R olling over the crashing waves as he nears
E ver looking for where he's gone
A nd at the end when there's no hope
M y eyes snap open and my mum is there in front of me!

Tyler Matthew Moore (8)
Malmesbury CE Primary School, Tetbury Hill

A Wizarding Realm

'Night,' I say when I go to bed
I rest my eyes and lay my head,
Deep in my dreams my thoughts will flow
The excitement of my dreams will go.

Wizards, spells and witches too,
Can create an illusion just for you
Happiness and fear are the emotions I feel
It really seems so very real.

Then I wake up from my dream,
I can't remember, it seems so mean
Up I get to start the day,
I hope I remember, come what may.

Poppy Wadsworth (10)
Malmesbury CE Primary School, Tetbury Hill

Buttercup

I open my eyes, what do I see?
A cute little puppy chasing a bee.
I look around,
I see a pound,
Full of cute little puppies.

The puppy stopped to stare at me
He looked as happy as can be
A warm feeling filled my heart
I never want to be apart
I said, 'This puppy is the one for me!'

I picked him up,
This is the pup.
I ran to the man
To ask if I can
Take him home with me, my Buttercup!

Isabel Carrick (9)
Malmesbury CE Primary School, Tetbury Hill

The Attack

Scared, out of breath
Shaking with my heart pounding.
Smoke fills the air, fire burning houses and trees all
around me,
People running past screaming, running for their lives.
Not moving, crouching, hiding, hoping they don't
see us.
Huge metal robots, with red evil eyes,
Shoot bullets and lasers from their hands
Decepticons trying to take over the Earth.
I'm scared, really scared
I think I'm going to die!

Bailey Wicks (10)
Malmesbury CE Primary School, Tetbury Hill

I'm Alone

I was alone, what should I do?
I didn't know where to go
I was in the forest alone and scared,
I called for help but nobody cared.
Suddenly, I heard my name,
So I tried my best to follow the voice,
And then I saw my mum!

Isabel Norman (9)
Malmesbury CE Primary School, Tetbury Hill

Daydreams

D uring maths I had a dream

A preposterous dream about food

Y ummy salty bananas and tasty chocolate tomatoes

D elicious bubblegum cheese and lovely berry potatoes

R eally it was weird!

E xcellent pretty nachos and explosive tuna jam

A mazing fiery carrots and mouth-watering strawberry ham.

M rs Wyatt shouted, 'Wake up, it's lunchtime!'

Henry Young (8)
Malmesbury CE Primary School, Tetbury Hill

Fishing With Grandad

F ishing is full of fun

I sit and wait for it to take my bait

S itting with Grandad brings lots of joy, all that's left is to catch a koi

H elp! I fall in the river, never mind I'll sit and shiver

I n and out the bushes as I go

N ot a lot happening, I must change my bait before it's too late

G reat big fish on my line, I changed bait just in time!

Josh Slade (8)
Malmesbury CE Primary School, Tetbury Hill

Food Fight Dream

In a dream I had last night
Two boys wanted a food fight
They flew in their very own plane
To a shop that was completely insane
The shop was filled with doughnuts and cupcakes
They were really yummy bakes
They bought the bakes with pockets of money
Then set up ready expecting it to be really funny
The boys were covered in chocolate and gooey cream
This was a great dream!

Milo Chilman (9)
Malmesbury CE Primary School, Tetbury Hill

Dreams

D reamland is almost here, nightmares, so full of fear
R eal things come into your mind, what things will you find?
E vil dreams give you a fright, wake up suddenly, you just might
A re you paddling in a pool? The water feels really cool
M aybe you feel danger, being chased by a stranger
S afely back in your bed, all snuggled up with Ted.

Declan Rice (9)
Malmesbury CE Primary School, Tetbury Hill

Scary Clown

Along through the night,
I had a little fright.
It was a creepy clown,
that gave me a frown.
The clown was holding a scarecrow
It was not over yet.
There was a gloomy alleyway,
That led to a jet.
The jet made the dream end,
the night is over.
I'm safe home in bed,
So bye, got to go and get my brekkie.
It was all in my head.

Matthew Norman (9)
Malmesbury CE Primary School, Tetbury Hill

Hidden In The Dark

Fairies dance in the sky,
Don't stare in their eye,
As it turns midnight,
He is gone by midnight.

Vroom! goes the cars,
The silence is now ours,
Mysterious bugs all around,
With the sound of *owww!*

Now he is lost,
Now he is gone,
For all that I know,
He will be dead from now!

Chloe Carol Kuchczynski (9)
Malmesbury CE Primary School, Tetbury Hill

Unicorn Race

U nicorn please take me on a ride

N orth, south, east or west

I don't mind, or through the countryside

C arry on going, don't stop!

O ver the mountains and rainbows so high

R osemary and I have so much fun, through the clouds and over the rainbow

N ever hurt a unicorn or it will get mad.

Freya Willis (9)
Malmesbury CE Primary School, Tetbury Hill

Unicorns Above The Clouds

Once I met a unicorn
That had a glimmering horn.
And said, 'Nacky, nacky, nack, nack!'
Which meant get on my back.
We flew back to Rainbow Land
And coming back, we did land.
We saw clouds and went to them
And on the clouds it was a dream come true...
Would it be a dream come true for you?

Eloise Wilson (9)
Malmesbury CE Primary School, Tetbury Hill

My Dream Life

M y dream is rapid,
Y ou are in it,

D ream away
R un your dream
E xciting time
A lot of fun
M um and Dad are awake

L ight the room until it's bright
I f you spot a unicorn
F orget about the morning
E at a dream life.

Jodie Sarine Foster (9)
Malmesbury CE Primary School, Tetbury Hill

On The Sea

I was on a boat watching the crashing sea
As my dad drank black coffee.
The waves crashed as other stuff tipped over,
And went bash as water came in,
Everyone panicked and grabbed a thing,
People could hear the birds sing,
Everyone went silent as the ship sank
As I woke up and said, 'Good, it was only a dream!'

Joseph Sladden (8)
Malmesbury CE Primary School, Tetbury Hill

Singing

S howing the crowd who you really are

I nspiring my friends and family

N oticing the cheering going around

G iving a great performance

I magine the whole world listening to your music

N ever hitting the wrong notes

G etting a big applause at the end of the performance.

Ben Templer (10)
Malmesbury CE Primary School, Tetbury Hill

Famous Me

F lashing at me,
A mazing dress with jewels on I'm wearing
M y hair is crimped
O n the red carpet I stand
U nexpectedly I see Taylor Swift
S miling and waving at the crowd.

M y emotion is...
E xcited!

Laura Tate (9)
Malmesbury CE Primary School, Tetbury Hill

How My Mummy Doesn't Like A Dummy

My mummy hates those dummy things,
That ventriloquists use,
She doesn't like their staring eyes,
Or their small, tiny shoes,
When she sees those dummy things,
It makes her give a scream,
In this nightmare of a vision,
A dark and lonely dream.

Harry Jacob White (8)
Malmesbury CE Primary School, Tetbury Hill

Dreams

D reams are mysterious and magic but

R andom nightmares can be a tricky job

E nding dreams can make you happy or sad

A nd you should never give up on them

M ost of all dreams make me happy and when you're happy you are unstoppable.

Rosie Katya Coode (10)
Malmesbury CE Primary School, Tetbury Hill

Sticky, Sticky

Sticky, sticky, I waded through toffee,
Then there was something choccy.

I looked up at the candy cane tree,
And then went to look at the lemonade sea.

Fizz, fizz, running over sherbet sand,
And I swam to a minty island.

Joseph Kirkman (9)
Malmesbury CE Primary School, Tetbury Hill

Unicorn And Panda = Pandacorn

I saw a unicorn,
Who had a long horn.
He was on a quest,
To find a panda who was best,
At eating bamboo shoots,
But sometimes he likes to eat very juicy fruits
I asked where he was going to,
China is where pandas live, but there is only a few.

Emily Holt (10)
Malmesbury CE Primary School, Tetbury Hill

Dream

D own on the golf course I hit the perfect shot

R apidly the ball spins through the air

E xcellent shot, it lands on the green, the crowd go wild

A n excellent putt, I win the Masters

M asters green jacket I have it at last.

James William Legg (9)
Malmesbury CE Primary School, Tetbury Hill

Dreaming

D aylight no longer present
R emembering the days gone by
E verlasting memories
A lways on my mind
M oments to treasure
I magining being there on a
N ever-ending quest
G one are the days.

Charlie Hancock (9)
Malmesbury CE Primary School, Tetbury Hill

Our Planet

Our planet, Planet Earth
Is it ours, and what is it worth?

I would like to save all the trees.
All the animals and especially bees.

So let's all save Planet Earth.
Because it is our planet, for what it's worth.

Macy May Ford (8)
Malmesbury CE Primary School, Tetbury Hill

Dreams

D reaming takes me somewhere new
R ound the track in a racing car
E very race I win by far
A nd now I am a champion
M cLaren want me on their team!
S hame I awake before I agree...

Edward Lane (9)
Malmesbury CE Primary School, Tetbury Hill

Flying

Flying, flying in the sky
Come and join me and have a try
Seeing flowers, seeing sky
We're on an adventure up, up high
Rainbow-coloured ladybirds
Ponies, unicorns and singing birds.

Rosemary Joan Robins (9)
Malmesbury CE Primary School, Tetbury Hill

Fairies

F luttering above the trees

A mazing sight to see,

I can't believe my eyes

R ound the pixie tree

Y es, yes, yes beautiful as can be.

Lily Harris (9)
Malmesbury CE Primary School, Tetbury Hill

Hot-Air Balloon Disaster

I rode in a hot-air balloon nice and wide.
Small and tidy all the time
I crashed one day, it ended with death
And then I was in the newspaper like Taylor Swift.

Fiona Hunt (9)
Malmesbury CE Primary School, Tetbury Hill

I Leap Into My Dream

I leap into my dream
I read it out of my mind
Stops and turns and wondrous things
A scary one, a frightful night
But am I in charge of my dream?

Samuel Davies (9)
Malmesbury CE Primary School, Tetbury Hill

Daydream

One hour down yet five more to go,
My pencil case looked like a pillow
And silently told myself that
I would close my eyes for a minute or two,
Well, wouldn't you?
I opened my eyes and stood up only to find,
An astonishing giraffe in the middle of a hot
sandy desert.
With peach-coloured fur and eyes like a rose,
And don't get me started on his short stout nose,
We both stood upright
And jumped in fright,
Then our mouths dropped in awe
As we saw...
A beautiful house with flowers climbing up the wall.
The sweet smell of nectar rushed up my eager nose,
I suddenly heard my name being chanted louder and
louder...
Bang!
The teacher told me off for daydreaming,
It was an amazing feeling,
If only it was real...

Lauren Howe (10)
Mitton Manor Primary School, Tewkesbury

Magical World

It was the start of the school day
this time no ideas to dream it away
If only I had got out of bed
but I wanted to rest my sleepy head
I could have watched TV
to give some ideas to me
I walked through the door,
feeling no galore.
Hung up my bag and my coat
leaving behind my billy goat
I walked into the classroom
feeling the unhappy gloom.
I sat down at my desk,
like a lovely pest.
A child was shouting in my ear
but I didn't hear,
I didn't even care
that he was pulling my hair.
When I opened my eyes
to my surprise,
I was in a house
staring at a mouse,
he said his name was Ninja,
although he was ginger.

The house was like a golden castle
and by the window I heard a rustle
by surprise to see before my very eyes
I saw a magic unicorn
with a magic horn
Suddenly noises running through my mind
I thought I must be blind
I opened my eyes
and to my surprise
I was back at school
with my friends playing the fool.

Amber Keightley (10)
Mitton Manor Primary School, Tewkesbury

Mysterious Wonderland

Come back, Miss Unicorn
I saw you last night
I crawled through waving candyfloss to see your horn
And they were full of colour and light.

I am starting to see the beautiful land
It is appearing in my eyes
You gave me your hand
I know you would not lead me to lies.

Let me drift away with this calming sound
Let me ride into the sunset scene
I will lay on this ground
Until you let me see the green.

Finally, I can see your house
I love the way it looks
Unfortunately, it has a mouse
Like in all those fairy-tale books.

Holly Greening (10)
Mitton Manor Primary School, Tewkesbury

In Time

One day in class I fell asleep,
Hey, by the way, I'm Gracey just to say!
This might sound crazy!
But I am a bit lazy.
I woke up from my dream and this is what I see,
Lexi and Chase were staring at me,
We were in this gloomy place,
and in front of me was a haunted house that I
could see.
Thunder clapped and the sky did glow.
Inside the haunted house there was a time machine,
It was the biggest thing you could have ever seen
When I stepped I could see.
Zombies coming for me and suddenly I heard a sound,
it was the super loud end of class bell.

Brooke Keay (10)
Mitton Manor Primary School, Tewkesbury

Flying Boat Lands On The Moon

My friends were at the park with me
We had a tremendous idea
A flying boat to Mars
We would need a hard-working team.

A bright white boat dancing to the rocking waves
The white boat transformed
Into a blinding flying boat with took all our might.

We shall fly away on some luxurious seats
And we will hear the music beat
The engine roared as we took off
Happily, the boat danced in space with a
white glimmer.

We landed on Mars
The stars were surrounding
We all mumbled in surprise
Whilst Earth rumbled.

Jake Rowden (10)
Mitton Manor Primary School, Tewkesbury

Magic

As the train starts on the track,
I can hear the clickety-clack.

Me and my friends scream yes,
Then we see a huge mess.

There are sheep,
Emma starts to weep.

We suddenly see the house,
Sophie squeaks like a mouse.

We all jump off
Then I start to cough.

We have fun and duel together,
We'll be friends forever and ever.

When nights fall,
We play and have a ball.

And when we wake up,
We're ready to start again!

Phoebe Kinsey (10)
Mitton Manor Primary School, Tewkesbury

The Magic Unicorn

The grass is lime green
And the trees are dark brown.
Wow so many jelly beans
I start to get excited and walk with my unicorn.
And my furry, cute little friend
I love the colours on my unicorn's horn.
Then we come to a bend
'Oh my look!' says my furry friend.
Whoever has a house like this?
From now on I have to look for bends
Everywhere here is bliss...
Then she woke up with a fright.
And realised it was the middle of night
The dream was so deep.
Until she drifted slowly back to sleep.

Evie Marie Rowlands (10)
Mitton Manor Primary School, Tewkesbury

The Dream Of No Other

When I went to sleep last night I had a dream like
no other,
And when I woke up the next morning everything
was different!
All I used to care about was food and now it is dance!
I dance all day every day, now I know how much I
like it,
I dance and dance and dance some more until I get
puffed out,
It's near the end of the day now and I just got home
from dance,
It was the best time ever,
The day is finally over and I am in bed.
And when I woke up the next morning everything was
back to normal!

Robyn Smith (9)
Mitton Manor Primary School, Tewkesbury

Unicorns

Fern-green forest lovers,
Sickly eight-legged spider haters,
Wonderful animal carers,
Distant dream discoverers,
Leafy dancing tree hugger,
Dastardly devastation stoppers,
Almost extinct extreme protectors,
Fantasy fairy dancers,
Blooming flower growers,
Curly candy cloud jumpers,
Terribly troubled reproducers,
Flowing rainbow hair owners,
Flaming hooves holders,
Great grass warriors,
Heartful, human healers,
Mighty zoo savers,
Lazy relaxers,
Green thumb planters.

Megan Rainbow (10)
Mitton Manor Primary School, Tewkesbury

Magical Garden

When I opened my eyes I saw unicorns
My friends and I kept walking by.
We saw lots of different coloured horns
I wonder what else we'll spy?

As I jumped upon the unicorn's back
We galloped around and then did a trot.
Suddenly, the speed started to lack
I mentioned a break as it was getting hot.

Finally to end the day,
Us and the unicorns decided to play.
Before we left we fed the unicorns some hay
Now we have to leave, but I wish we could stay.

Hannah Dyke (10)
Mitton Manor Primary School, Tewkesbury

The Magical Forest

I can see an elf,
Sitting on a shelf.
A unicorn eating grass,
A dragon learning brass.
When I take another step,
And I see a fairy prepare her children's lunch for
school?
An evil Giant Grumble,
A dinosaur ready to rumble.
Monsters with one eye,
Then I see an elf eating apple pie.
A unicorn with a horn,
A fairy just been born.
My friend the gingerbread man and I getting
into trouble,
We make a pretty cheeky double.

Holly Stark (9)
Mitton Manor Primary School, Tewkesbury

The Dragon

One minute I was lying in bed
The next I was out dressed in red!
At least I still had Rosie
Although I didn't feel cosy
Outside like this with Rosie by my side
I sat down watching the tide
Until I ended up hopping on a wagon
Wait, was that a dragon?
It was coming at me with lightning speed
I really only wanted to read!
Why did I have to wear red?
Then suddenly I woke up back in bed!

Wil Redfern (10)
Mitton Manor Primary School, Tewkesbury

The Golden Jaguar

Come home, golden jaguar.
I couldn't see your golden jewels this morning.
I searched the town and battled the freezing
cold snow,
And that gave me a shock you know,
Giving me comfort with your amazing golden jewels.
When I see them you make the bad dreams go away.
The clouds are clearing I hope you're close.
I see your jewels finally you're here.
Hip hip hooray!

Amelia Hyldon (10)
Mitton Manor Primary School, Tewkesbury

Life On Mars

I had a dream
That I was flying
As I had a fear of dying.
When we landed
I felt that
I was stranded
But then I saw
A lovely door
And so many more.
And I thought Earth
was all a bore
Pass it down to the one before.
But where are these people
Are they at the steeple
Wherever they are
They must have a car
No you say
I'll come back one day.

Katie Wheeler (10)
Mitton Manor Primary School, Tewkesbury

Candy Land

One night I fell asleep
And woke up in Candy Land.
With candy as far as the eye can see,
With chocolate huts scattered around.

There was a large hut on the top of toffee hill,
Inside were three clowns called Hop, Hip and Pip.
They were three party animals
Suddenly everything went wavy and I woke up in
my bedroom.

Thomas Clements (9)
Mitton Manor Primary School, Tewkesbury

Unicorn Wonderland

Mystical creatures
Human enchanters
Beauty holders
Pink weaners
Mint likers
Chocolate eaters
Magic makers
Secret flyers
Picnic lovers
Cloud dancers
Proud species
Forest walkers
Crowd haters
Delicate consumers
Quiet relaxers
Race runners
Spider dislikers.

Evie Chambers (10)
Mitton Manor Primary School, Tewkesbury

Unicorn's Nightmare

Sky runner
Cloud chaser
Flying higher
Space invader
Lost founder
Scary shelter
Creepy owner
Dark winter
Open barrier
Getting closer
Appearing darker
Gigantic sparkler
Cliffs closer
Falling quicker
Scary dreamer
Heavy sleeper.

Sophie Parker (10)
Mitton Manor Primary School, Tewkesbury

Sweet Secret Garden

Happy gardener
Mystery writer
Sweet lover
Grass fluffer
Wind dancer
Chocolate licker
Beauty holder
Birds happier
Lake colder
Gate squeaker
Picnic enjoyer
Cloud dancer.

Evie Lawley (9)
Mitton Manor Primary School, Tewkesbury

Once Upon A Dream

Hail, wind and thunder, *boom!*
I fall back and crash my head onto the murky ground.
I hear a distant, hypnotic buzz.
Screeches and yells, where am I?

The waft of wet, damp leaves surround me.
My feet are lavished in bugs who are biting me,
like vampires craving my blood.
I am their prey.
Some flying, some speeding behind me,
Ladybugs, mutant ladybugs!
It is a chase now, I run as fast as I can.
But no, they catch up with me!
My legs start to ache and go all floppy,
Pain grips my knees, they are going to collapse!
There is no hope, I can't carry on any more...

I wake up,
It must have been a nightmare.
Images fade.
I am now back in my cosy bed,
But it all felt so real, it can't be, can it?
Ouch! A sharp pain stings my ankle.

Tentatively, I pull back my duvet... to reveal a plague of angry sores.
They are spreading rapidly beyond my knees, evolving into spherical midnight-black spots!

Elsa Bearman (10)
Shrivenham CE Primary School, Shrivenham

A Starlit Dream

I step on the stars
The sky is black.
It fills my head with imagination

I feel like I'm floating,
Yet my feet are held by the stars.
They make a path, taking me where
I do not know.

I am excited
I am scared.
How can this be?

Am I asleep? Am I awake?
I really just don't know.

I see a flash of lightning
I wake up in my bed.
I realise it's just a dream
Going on inside my head.

Flora Waymouth (8)
Shrivenham CE Primary School, Shrivenham

My Pet Dragon

My ferocious big red dragon,
He got stuck in his old dusty wagon.

Black eyes with flicks of gold,
Eats his food with bits of mould.

He flies high, high up in the sky,
He comes down when the weather is dry.

His tongue is long, his tail is strong,
He has spikes down his back and collects his treasure
in his sack.

Until one day,
He had flown away.

But never was he seen again.

Arun Dhoot (9)
Shrivenham CE Primary School, Shrivenham

Danger In The Sea

The sparkling, aqua-blue sea
Sun shining from up high
Seaweed waving and squirming.

Clouds pass by in slow motion
Fish scream, dark bubbles,
Clownfish giggle, giggle.
The shark is heading our way
All he wants is to play.

Not for long
He gobbles us up
In a flash of light and bubbles
The good thing is no more trouble.

Charlie Taylor (9)
Shrivenham CE Primary School, Shrivenham

My Dream

First by the river
Then by the sea
Seven silver fish folk
Swam up to me.

Jumping in the water
My legs turned to fins
Zooming through the ocean
I began to swim.

My friends were all creatures
From the deep, deep blue
It was such a lovely dream
I wish it could be true.

Nyah Harmer (8)
Shrivenham CE Primary School, Shrivenham

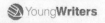

Myths

Magical, magical creatures these are,
Yetis, unicorns, wizards and monsters,
They roam around these places.
Help! They start to chase me!
Suddenly, I wake to find myself in bed!

Daniel Chaston (8)
Shrivenham CE Primary School, Shrivenham

The World Of Dance

It was twelve o'clock and I was in my bed,
My adorable puppy lying ahead.
I could see outside a bejewelled sky,
At that moment I wished I could fly.

Like a parachute a star began to fall,
And it fell right on my outside stool!
I cautiously began to walk over to it,
Then all of a sudden I ungracefully tripped.

My body felt tingly with excitement,
All of a sudden I could see a present.
Suddenly I heard a *bang!* And the star began
to explode,
It opened a portal where a unicorn rode!

I saw green vines jumping on a dance floor,
I did a walkover and revealed a door!
I skipped in, my unicorn with me,
Suddenly I began to see...

A fairy teaching people how to pirouette!
I saw my puppy tangled in a net.
Suddenly I heard my mum shouting, 'You'll be late
for school!'
Then I realised I had dreamt it all.

Bonnie Davies (9)
Stonar School, Atworth

Candy Land

Going to sleep is a very big bug,
Tossing and turning in my big rug,
Dreaming and dreaming about everything,
Candy lands, chocolate, sweets and kings.

I'm in a big candy land with people all around,
Everything's made of sweets and chocolate, even
the hound,
Not even allowed to go outside because it is
too dangerous,
But I am a very very big girl who's adventurous.

My best friend dragon, who cries nice sweets,
My best friend ever so we have to share treats,
'Why don't we just run away from home?'
'Yes, okay but we can't just go and roam.'

'Open the window and get outside,
You don't want your little sister to spy,'
Sweets all around us, sweets everywhere,
Golden pillars made of chocolate and a bear!

Oh no, the Bon Bon bear is very scary,
Fight, fight, kill, kill the fairies,
The Bon Bons and the fairies,
Are very scary, their leader is Mary.

I'm very sad because it's time to go,
As my mum shouts my name, 'Chloe!'
Just one more second in candy land
I can't bear to go back to the city that is bland.

Laura Sparrow (9)
Stonar School, Atworth

World War Two

I had a dream, a dream to become a detective.
As my head rested on the pillow, a dream flooded my brain,
I heard a howl at the moon and then a gunshot as it sounded,
I opened my window and climbed out onto the ivy.

I climbed down and down,
Down and down I went,
My feet suddenly banged on the gravel-covered driveway!
I walked through the woodland drive that was all dark and I felt worried.

I looked up at the stunning and shimmering bright moon,
I opened the gold and black gates that made a bright reflection,
On the dark, muddy field.
I walked through the gates and onto the country road.

There was a short, small and stubby shadow walking towards me,
I walked closer to it and through the gates.
I screamed.
The small shadow had jumped onto me!

I awoke in a dark room,
It was really crowded with short people,
Then I realised where I was.
I was in hospital.

More people crowded around me and started talking in
small whispers.
People with lovely grey cameras were clicking away
at me,
My mum was standing with the nurse and chatting.
I wished that my dad could be here but sadly he is
fighting in World War Two.

Suddenly I was whooshed into a dark black portal,
And was being pulled back to my world,
I was not happy,
I landed with a thump on my bed.

It was raining.
The rain was running down my window at quite a pace,
I suddenly wished the war would be *over!*
And that my dad could come home to my family.

Isabella Beatrice Chadwick (9)
Stonar School, Atworth

The Linked Dream

When I get home with Jennifer for a
fantastic sleepover,
We eat a *scrumdidleompous* dinner.
And talk about horses and sing and dance,
We get to bed and dream away to a different place.

Whoosh, zoom! We are in a mystical world far
from here,
We dream away passed giant country, we go far away.
We link dreams like lemon drops and disappear,
We see our magical pals and the candyfloss
trees singing.

Our pals Star, Twinkle, Shimmer and Shine are fairies,
That are pink and blue.
Magic and Marshmallow are twin unicorns,
They have glittery horns and fur as white as snow
That feels as soft as marshmallows
Our dragons, Toothy and Stormy, are both
different kinds.

This place was made out of diamonds, food
and seashells,
The ocean and the magic crystal was covered in
black goo.

Then Magic and Marshmallow came up to us and
didn't look happy,
Something was wrong, I knew it all along.

The evil witch, the evil witch she wore a black coat,
with a black hat and a green and blue dress and a wart
on her throat.
She steals magic things, to have more power
soon she'll rule the world...
The linked dream!

How are we going to stop her?
Shine was busy talking to the milkshake lake.
We listened for a little while,
Unfortunately before we could do anything...
It was morning!
'Wakey wakey, rise and cakey!' called my mum with
a giggle,
My mum's got really pretty hazelnut eyes
And black with gold streaks of hair.
'Come on, up you get, time for dance class!'

Poppy May Sumner (9)
Stonar School, Atworth

Once Upon A Killer Clown

I went to bed because I was tired,
And suddenly I heard a flying gunshot being fired,
I had a dream about a killer clown,
And he was chasing me all around.

I went running around the laughing house,
And suddenly I saw a squeaking mouse,
I screamed and hopped over it,
And then suddenly the clown slipped.

I went into a room with a wizard in it,
He was very slim and had a lot of kit,
He was making lovely poison spells,
Inside of steaming hot wishing wells.

Suddenly I woke up with a fright,
And then I saw a bright shine of light,
I just realised it was a dream,
And suddenly I heard my sister scream...

Lilly Cherry (9)
Stonar School, Atworth

Pheoland

I was not prepared for this land I see,
Bubbling volcanoes and a blood-red sea.
Fizzing with action are angry clouds of lightning,
And in the sky, pheonixes fly, looking quite frightening.

Excitement builds up in me, I love this mythical land,
And I hear the legendary Pheocand, the best ever
Phoenix band.
At that exact moment, a phoenix swoops by,
And I watch him fly towards me, soaring through
the sky.

Suddenly without a warning, he grabs me in his talons,
And near a fire mountain he drops me into a cavern.
With a *thud!* I land, my body feeling dead,
Within moments I wake up to find I'm safe at home
in bed!

Emma Louise Skinner (9)
Stonar School, Atworth

Starcraft Miracle

I went to sleep and started dreaming,
I went to Blizzcon to a tournament,
I was playing with Lowko in archon mode,
Four champions, we were doing well on our economy,
Our defences medium, army low,
When we had a siege we used our forces to defend,
It was a giant success.

We defended our base and we got a giant army
to attack,
Then we attacked but we were ambushed,
We survived against their zerg ambush
We were still attacking,
We destroyed their defences,
Our army died but another was coming,
We held it back, I had a tingly feeling,
I felt that they were doing an air raid,
Out of the corner of my eye,
I saw three mutalisks heading towards us.

Our missile turrets aimed and fired rapidly to kill them,
Just then I saw a zergling swarm with efficient speed,
Rushing through the rushing surface we put four siege
tanks in place,
And marines killing the most zerglings,

Then we destroyed their base me and Lowko...
But I heard my mum say,
'Wake up, it's almost time for school!'

Michael Ross Matthew MacLeod (9)
Stonar School, Atworth

Stardust The Stolen Unicorn

When I went to bed that night,
I saw a flicker of light,
Next I saw a magical unicorn,
When I saw her, she had a newborn.

When I looked back there was nothing there,
All I could see was dust in the hot air,
Next I saw a graceful fairy,
Like a sleepy lion, I was very weary.

The fairy came before the dawn
To save Stardust the unicorn, wrapped in thorns,
But she was nowhere to be seen
The monster has taken her in her dreams.

Just then I saw Stardust running towards us,
She was galloping as fast as a bus
The horrible monster was running behind her
With teeth as big as a black, mean jaguar.

The monster said that he'll get us when we least
expect it,
I hope a swarm of bees sting him in a bit!
He is driving away in his monster truck
So let's get him on our bikes and catch him, wish
us luck!

Eva Norman (9)
Stonar School, Atworth

134

The World Of Horses

I see people galloping a cross-country site,
I'm at a jump with total fright,
I see people coming at top speed,
They are coming towards me in smart tweed.

My fussy mum says, 'Get more intelligent,
If you don't I will call the president!
Hurry up it's getting very, very late,
Hurry up it's number eight.'

A child falls off as gracefully as a peacock,
Me and my mum are in total shock,
I run round like a headless chicken,
Then I see a little kitten.

When the little pony is out of the way,
Here comes Pinto singing to save the day,
When all of a sudden everything blurs,
Then my eyes start flickering as I stir.

Like a frightened mouse I wake up,
Then my sister says, 'What's up?'
Her jump is very extreme,
Then I realise it was all a dream.

Phoebe Tombs (8)
Stonar School, Atworth

The Dragon Dream

I was in my bed one night.
And it gave me quite a fright.
And when I went to bed.
Something went wrong with my head.

And when I woke up everything looked different.
Even though it looked quite current.
When I looked up in the sky I saw a dragon.
Soaring by.

Then it landed with a thump.
And dumped me near a rubbish dump.
Then the world turned upside down.
Then I began to frown.
Then I woke up and everything looked different.

Oliver Newman (8)
Stonar School, Atworth

The Gummo Dino

I went to sleep and I...
Started to dream about Dino
And the first thing I thought about
Was a big greedy, strange rhino
But then I thought about a big,
Humongous and efficient Gummo Dino.

I was with my brother
And his name is Louis
He always keeps pooing
A humongous, gigantic poo
He went to the nearest dinosaur pond,
And it was so blue.

Oliver Deakin (9)
Stonar School, Atworth

Dream Land

In Dream Land, a normal day, a normal town and
normal school...
But is it really a normal day?
I start to act like a fool!
By whispering to my friends.
My teacher asks, 'What did Issy say?'
I reply, 'I don't know!'
'Off to Mrs Scutt's, this is no time to play!
Lily, I can't believe that you can't behave!'
Out of the corner of my eye,
I see a rusty old machine under a cream blanket...
I must be brave!
I quickly crawl inside.
A button turns green and starts to countdown...
Five... four... three... two... one... and I'm off!

I'm in a sweet town.
Everything is covered in sugary sweets.
This dream is hard to beat!
There are sweets from my head to my feet.
A humongous factory floats past on a candyfloss
cloud.

I jump up inside
I get a life-lasting gobstopper

I've finished my journey,
Off we go!
I suddenly wake up
I'm back in my bed.

Lily Jennings (9)
Stow On The Wold Primary School, Stow On The Wold

My Alicorn

In a river of candyfloss and marshmallows
I am riding on an alicorn.
I can hear the sound of squelchy marshmallows.
I can see on the horns of my alicorn,
There is the sticky but fluffy candyfloss stuck tight.
In the river of candyfloss and marshmallows,
We jump over the chocolate falls
And land in Fudge-Forest River,
In the land of Fudge-Forest River
We soar above the rooftops,
Landing in the garden of the gingerbread man's house.
We knock on the Wispa Gold door.
Inside we can see a gingerbread man
With chocolate smudges on his face.
In the Land of Fudge-Forest,
The gingerbread man does not want to speak,
So we go on...
We fly to the Jungle of Fruits.
In the Jungle of Fruits, it's as colourful as a rainbow.
We enter the Jungle of Fruits
And we meet a friendly monkey

Who gives us a backpack full of useful things to say thank you
For when we untangled his tail off the vicious bramble bush.

Maggie Brain (8)
Stow On The Wold Primary School, Stow On The Wold

Is It Really A Dream?

Ploughing a field
A tractors JCB with filthy tyres.
Skidding around corners.
Is it really a dream?
As night falls a beam of light appears.
Back to the farm.
It's raining mud.
The cows are stampeding to the gate.
They think I've got some food.
They move backwards thinking I'm opening the gate.
I scuttle back to the lime-green truck.
I put it into reverse, I'm speeding backwards, I
nearly crash!
I turn round and speed up the track
I get out the truck
It's starting to rain
I put my mac on my back
This is really a pain!
I'm walking to the main entrance with my trusty dog.

Oliver Hicks (8)
Stow On The Wold Primary School, Stow On The Wold

Ocean Dream

I hear beautiful flowing waves that flow down into
my dreams,
When I get there,
I can see octopuses that are sleeping calmly,
It's like they have had a cup of chamomile tea.
I touch the beautiful octopuses,
It looks like a rose gold flower.
I am as spine-tingling as a humongous
fire-breathing dragon,
I am on my own, what if it stings me?
The lovely ocean goes deeper and deeper
You go into the silver water,
That comes from the ocean of dreams,
It has tropical fish, swimming like a big hurricane.
They run like an Olympic swimmer away from their
predator.

Madisen Keyte (9)
Stow On The Wold Primary School, Stow On The Wold

F1 Experience

In my dream
I see tight corners and long straights
It's hard to concentrate.
I'm zooming along
In Formula One
With Sebastian Vettel
Chasing my metal
It's pouring with rain
Here in Bahrain.
I hear a strange noise
Coming from the back
It's my best friend, Ben
And his dog, Jack
I'm so excited
I drive off the track
Oh no!
I think I broke my back
I wake up from my dream
I can't believe what I've seen
I've actually driven a Ferrari Formula One machine!

Luke Michael Smith (8)
Stow On The Wold Primary School, Stow On The Wold

In Fairy Land

I see fairies around me.
Trees, flowers, sunshine.
Waking me up in the middle of the night
feeling excited.
My imaginary friends are Ruby and Liljana.
I'm in Fairy Land if you didn't know.
I feel amused, happy, overjoyed.
Fairies fly around me collecting treasures
And jewels around the magnificent Fairy Land.
Like a beautiful butterfly.
Sprinting like a racehorse.
Blossom trees shine like crystals.
Where are we? I know!
We are in Fairy Land of course!

Amelia Liljana Ruby Taylor (8)
Stow On The Wold Primary School, Stow On The Wold

Space Poem

In space I saw ten whizzing
And whirling alien ships destroying a planet.

One chip and jelly rocker with a cherry on top,
Heading into a huge black hole like someone eating
a chip.

Two asteroids crashing like two tigers fighting
for meat.

One alien invasion heading to Earth to destroy
Every single ocean, then nasty pirates steal
the treasure.

Two dead unicorns shooting black holes
destroying planets.

Edward Nicholds-Brown (8)
Stow On The Wold Primary School, Stow On The Wold

Dream Land

I was in Dream Land, everything was lovely and edible.
I was happy but a bit afraid.

Then in the Dream Land a dangerous clown appeared.
So I hurried away as fast as I could.

Suddenly I was flying through the Dream Land.
I saw a chocolate river flowing along silently.

Eventually I lost the clown.
When I woke I told my family all about my dream!

Lexi Ellen Huckson (8)
Stow On The Wold Primary School, Stow On The Wold

In The Land Of The Amazon

In the land of dreams
A colossal tree is just standing there.
In the colossal tree
Beautiful birds squawk
To each other.
The ferocious tigers growl at the insane monkeys.
That is terribly annoying.
Whopping great big crocodiles.
Snapping at the leaping frog.

Issy Bayliss (8)
Stow On The Wold Primary School, Stow On The Wold

Animal Power Team

I see massive mouldy feet and mousetraps.
I'm with hamsters, lemmings, octopuses and rats
chasing us like cheetahs.

I am in a mansion
that is crashing down like a tent falling down!

Solly Bell (8)
Stow On The Wold Primary School, Stow On The Wold

My Debut For Manchester United

I am feeling nervous, as nervous as can be
I hear people chanting and they're chanting for me!

I am stood in the players' tunnel waiting for
the referee.
We are Manchester United's one and only team!

I walk onto the pitch with my manager Patrick.
Sixty minutes later I have scored a hat-trick!

I pass the ball to Rooney, who gets a penalty
I take the ball and score a goal,
My team look on with jealousy.

This is by far my best dream of all,
Because I scored all of the goals
And I got to take home the match ball!

Jacob Reed (8)
Sturminster Marshall First School, Sturminster Marshall

Night Dancers

N o one has ever heard of the prowling dancers or have they?

I f they knock on your door don't

G asp out loud!

H owever they hate light so that's how to make them invisible

T hen they will disappear!

D ancing wildly in the light of the moon...

A ttacking in the dark with only the moon shining glamorously

N o one should know about the night dancers...

C reeping and prancing to

E avesdrop on your conversation

R eady to scare you

S hadows in the dark!

Constance Springett (8)
Sturminster Marshall First School, Sturminster Marshall

Roald Dahl Dreaming

R eading Matilda transports me away

O rdinary dreams are not for today

A dventure Dream Country with the BFG

L aughing out loud in a peach with giant creatures

D elumptious Wonka chocolates are regular features

D angerous aunts like Spiker and Sponge

A fantastic fox takes a cider plunge

H orrible muckfrumping farmers are gunning

L ickswishing frobscottle - whizzpoppers coming!

Hana Brittain (7)
Sturminster Marshall First School, Sturminster Marshall

Spiders

S ilent hairy arachnids
P eople are terrified of them
I ncredible grip on the web
D ark corners are where they live.
E ating victims caught in their webs
R unning along the floor they go
S piders, spiders are everywhere.

James Mounty (8)
Sturminster Marshall First School, Sturminster Marshall

Dragons With Superpowers

D ragons with superpowers fly into my dream
R ed fiery laser eyes looking down at me
A ttack, attack!
G ang of dragons wants to eat me
O range, red, blue and green lasers shoot
N ow I'm going to die.

Edwyn White (8)
Sturminster Marshall First School, Sturminster Marshall

My Horse

How I love my little horse
I will brush her very well of course.
I will comb her tail and mane.
And go riding out again.

Freya Mabey (8)
Sturminster Marshall First School, Sturminster Marshall

Deep-Sea Diving

As I drift off
I dive into the sea of dreams.
As I dive deeper I find myself in a crystal-clear ocean.
Surrounded with bright vibrant fish
I breathe out expecting to inhale water,
But instead I see silvery bubbles float gracefully to
the surface.
I'm in deep-sea scuba gear.
Looking around to admire the coral reef around me.
I notice a hammerhead shark drifting peacefully over
my head,
With cleaner fish cleaning him of parasites and
dead scales.
Suddenly, a large stingray swims so close that
I can almost touch its smooth, soft, silk-like body.
Then I look at my air gauge
And I realise I don't have enough air to explore on.
So I start swimming to the surface
And find myself awake in my sea-blue bedroom.

Poppy Howarth-Barnes (11)
Westrop Primary School, Highworth

Unique Unicorns!

U nique lands awaited to be visited

N ever seeing a unicorn before, my jaw dropped wide open

I deas raced through my mind

C olourful fairies were riding the gorgeous creatures

O dd-shaped horns would sit on unicorn's heads

R unning quickly the beasts would pass by me

N ight skies were colourful when the unicorns were out

S tanding by the magnificent animal I thought to myself and said, 'I wish the magical creatures were real.'

Chloe May Jones (11)
Westrop Primary School, Highworth

Goblin Cave

The dark cave was huge,
Carefully walking, I stepped in.
In the shadows creeping,
A goblin waited for its food.
My heart thumped, *ba-boom!*
I was luckily dreaming!

Jamal Alan Frost (11)
Westrop Primary School, Highworth

YOUNG WRITERS INFORMATION

We hope you have enjoyed reading this book – and that you will continue to in the coming years.

If you're a young writer who enjoys reading and creative writing, or the parent of an enthusiastic poet or story writer, do visit our website **www.youngwriters.co.uk**. Here you will find free competitions, workshops and games, as well as recommended reads, a poetry glossary and our blog.

If you would like to order further copies of this book, or any of our other titles, then please give us a call or visit **www.youngwriters.co.uk**.

Young Writers
Remus House
Coltsfoot Drive
Peterborough
PE2 9BF
(01733) 890066
info@youngwriters.co.uk